today I affirm

A JOURNAL THAT NURTURES SELF-CARE

ALEXANDRA ELLE

Andrews McMeel
PUBLISHING®

Connect with Alexandra Elle

Instagram: @alex_elle
Twitter: @_alexelle
Website: alexelle.com

To share your affirmations on social media, use hashtag #1AffirmationADay.

Affirmations create space for us to relax, reflect, reset, and rearrange our personal narratives. If you've picked up this journal, perhaps you've been looking for a creative tool to help you with all of the above. Speaking life and kindness into our journeys opens the door of possibility through intentional language and self-care. The question that most people have is *how*. How do I start the process of not only writing but also meaning what I put down on paper? This journal was created with the *how* in mind. Writing, when done transparently and honestly, can serve as a form of meditation, therapy, and healing. When we slow down and settle into ourselves, positive self-affirmations can help build a home within by laying the foundation of self-awareness, introspection, and understanding.

Today I Affirm will walk you through the ins and outs of crafting positive self-talk in a way that is stress-free, relatable, and, hopefully, not overwhelming. Peeling back our emotional layers is an intense process, but we have the power to be our greatest teacher when we use writing as a self-reflection resource. Throughout these pages, you will find written examples of affirmations and opportunities to craft your own. Divided into sections, *Today I Affirm* has space to create affirmation charts and self-love letters. To assist you further in manifesting your self-care ritual, *Today I Affirm* is intertwined with journal prompts and quotes to get your mind moving and keep your heart open. Show up for yourself in these pages.

With Love,
Alexandra Elle

today I affirm

Journal Prompts

Answer these questions daily or as needed. Spend some time with each one and be intentional with the answers you provide. Once you've completed your answer, head to the bottom of the page and write an affirmation that corresponds with your journal prompt answer. I've given you an example on the following page, just in case you need some inspiration to get started.

Self-Care Teaches me that I can pour into myself just as much as I pour into others.

ALEX ELLE

SAMPLE ENTRY

1. What am I at this moment?

I am whole, even in the midst of struggles and hardships that feel like they can break me. I am learning that even during moments of adversity and confusion, I still have the power to own my journey and heal. Being ashamed of my truth isn't an option. My stories are mine. I will not be ashamed of my path or the things that threaten to shatter me. I am stronger than my hurt.

1. What am I at this moment?

_____

_____

_____

*give yourself
permission
to unfold, bloom,
and grow.*

2. Who do I want to become?

_____

_____

_____

Today I affirm _____

3. What fills me up with meaning and passion?

_____

_____

_____

4. In what ways do I need to shift in order to step into my higher self?

_____

_____

_____

Today I affirm _____

5. List five fears that are stopping you from moving forward.

6. How are you showing up for yourself?

_____

_____

_____

_____

Today I affirm _____

7. List five things that you want to rearrange in your life.

8. What excites you?

_____

_____

_____

Today I affirm _____

9. How can I step out of old bad habits in a way that is healthy, safe, and rooted in understanding?

_____

_____

_____

10. What do I want learn about myself? Dig deep.

_____

_____

_____

day I affirm _____

11. What do I need to step back from in order to see a clearer picture of what's around me?

_____

_____

_____

12. How can I relinquish control and still maintain peace over my life?

_____

_____

_____

Today I affirm _____

13. What am I scared of and how is my fear causing me to stay stuck?

_____

_____

_____

14. How am I settling into my healing in order to make room for growth?

_____

_____

_____

Today I affirm _____

15. List five things that you're grieving.

16. How am I greeting adversity with grace and understanding?

today I affirm

17. What leaves me feeling uneasy?

_____

_____

_____

18. How can I build better boundaries without feelings of guilt?

_____

_____

_____

Today I affirm _____

19. What and who am I shedding? Why?

_____

_____

_____

20. List at least twelve positive ways that you see yourself.

Today I affirm _____

21. List at least six negative ways that you see yourself.

22. How have I been let down in life?

_____

_____

_____

Today I affirm _____

23. In what ways am I learning to lift myself up and move forward in joy?

_____

_____

_____

24. List seven ways that you can tend your emotional garden and grow self-love.

Today I affirm _____

25. Who and what do you need to leave behind?

_____

_____

_____

Be patient with every part of your healing. There's no rush. Take your time.

26. Why is blooming essential for my end goal?

_____

_____

_____

Today I affirm _____

27. Am I hiding from myself? If so, how and why?

_____

_____

_____

28. What is my purpose?

_____

_____

_____

Today I affirm _____

29. How can I lead a life that is full of love, contentment, and resilience?

_____

_____

_____

30. List the things you need to let go of.

_____

_____

_____

Today I affirm _____

31. What do I need more of?

_____

_____

_____

32. What do I need less of?

_____

_____

_____

Today I affirm _____

33. What emotional clutter is causing chaos in my life?

_____

_____

_____

34. How does peace of mind allow me to show up for others and myself?

_____

_____

_____

today I affirm _____

35. List the ways you can release your shame.

_____

_____

_____

36. Is forgiveness hard for me?

_____

_____

_____

Today I affirm ——————————————————————

37. In what ways can I stand more firmly in my identity?

_____

_____

_____

38. How can I take control of my life, emotionally and physically?

_____

_____

_____

today I affirm ————————————————————

39. List the ways you've let yourself down.

_____

_____

_____

40. How can self-forgiveness take shape in my life?

_____

_____

_____

today I affirm _____

41. What does forgiveness (of self or others) feel like? Look like?

_____

_____

_____

42. What quiets my doubt and elevates my confidence?

_____

_____

_____

today I affirm _____

43. List your top five insecurities.

44. How can I unravel my truth?

_____

_____

_____

today I affirm _____

45. How can I nurture my joy?

_____

_____

_____

46. What is my path in life and how can I start walking on it?

_____

_____

_____

Today I affirm _____

47. In what ways am I strengthening the bond I have with myself?

_____

_____

_____

48. Do outside influences play a role in the speed or duration of my healing?

_____

_____

_____

Today I affirm ————————————————————

49. List the ways that you're doing the work to self-heal and self-preserve.

_____

_____

_____

Show up for yourself in ways no one else can. You are worthy.

50. List the reasons why you are enough.

_____

_____

_____

Today I affirm _____

51. In what ways am I lacking?

_____

_____

_____

52. Where can I make room for change in my life?

_____

_____

_____

Today I affirm _____

53. How am I being tested?

_____

_____

_____

54. In what ways can I learn from the adversity in my life?

_____

_____

_____

Today I affirm —————————————————————

55. What soothes my soul when things are chaotic?

_____

_____

_____

56. List five things that help you realign when you're thrown off track.

Today I affirm ⎯⎯⎯⎯⎯⎯⎯⎯⎯⎯⎯⎯⎯⎯⎯

57. Who in my life can I lean on when things get challenging?

_____

_____

_____

58. What qualities do I need in a support system?

_____

_____

_____

Today I affirm _____

59. List ten things that fill you up.

60. List ten things that deplete you.

Today I affirm ———————————————————

61. How can I surround myself with more of what uplifts my spirit?

_____

_____

_____

62. In what ways can I set boundaries that protect me from being drained emotionally?

_____

_____

_____

today I affirm _____

63. What breaks me down?

_____

_____

_____

64. What builds me up?

_____

_____

_____

Today I affirm _____

65. Am I happy where I am right now (job, love life, friendships, living situations, etc.)?

_____

_____

_____

66. What is my life's work?

_____

_____

_____

today I affirm _____

67. How do I see myself in this moment?

_____

_____

_____

68. What layers do I need to pull back in order to bloom?

_____

_____

_____

Today I affirm _____

69. Who do I need to forgive to tap into my emotional freedom and healing?

_____

_____

_____

70. List the five main stressors in your life.

Today I affirm _____

71. List five ways you can start living on your own terms.

72. Do I take authentic ownership of my joy?

Today I affirm ——————————————

73. How can I strengthen what I know to be true about my journey and relationships, and myself?

_____

_____

_____

Be mindful of your self-talk.
Be kind and gentle on
your journey.

74. What do I need to accept in order to heal?

_____

_____

_____

day I affirm _____

75. List ten things you are not defined by.

76. List ten things that make you who you are.

Today I affirm —————————————————

77. How am I taking shape in this season of my life?

_____

_____

_____

78. Am I wrapped up in my past in a way that is unhealthy?

_____

_____

_____

Today I affirm ————————————————————

79. Why do I struggle with relinquishing control?

_____

_____

_____

80. What makes you soft?

_____

_____

_____

Today I affirm _____

81. What makes you strong?

_____

_____

_____

82. What am I unpacking, keeping, and throwing away?

_____

_____

_____

Today I affirm _____

83. What type of relationships do I want to nourish in my life?

_____

_____

_____

84. What influences my sense of belonging?

_____

_____

_____

Today I affirm _____

85. How can I shed my shame?

_____

_____

_____

86. How do I own my truth in a way that makes me productive and safe?

_____

_____

_____

Today I affirm _____

87. What is my life's vision?

_____

_____

_____

88. Where do you hide your joy?

_____

_____

_____

today I affirm _____

89. Where do you find joy?

_____

_____

_____

90. Who taught you self-love?

_____

_____

_____

Today I affirm ——————————————————————

91. What goodness am I pouring into the world?

_____

_____

_____

92. What do I want in this moment?

_____

_____

_____

Today I affirm _____

93. List five ways you want to be loved.

94. List five reasons why you want to be heard.

Today I affirm —

95. How am I protecting my self-love?

_____

_____

_____

96. How am I honoring my boundaries?

_____

_____

_____

today I affirm _____

97. Define your magic.

_____

_____

_____

98. What am I committed to?

_____

_____

_____

Today I affirm _____

99. What is shaping my ability to transform and transcend?

_____

_____

_____

Own your entire story.

100. List your ten best qualities.

Today I affirm _____

I cannot change
the hurt of my past,
but I can decide to
stand tall in my healing
and march forward
with my lessons in
hand and heart intact.

ALEX ELLE

today I affirm

Affirmation Charting

Journaling can seem extremely out of reach for some. Many think that it calls for a "dear diary" experience, but it doesn't have to. Charting your affirmations is not only a fun spin on journaling, but it can also help get your thoughts out and organized without feeling like a heavy or unattainable task. See the example I've left for you and model yours after it if you need inspiration. The more you chart, the easier it becomes.

Self-love teaches
me that empathy,
compassion, and
showing up fully must
start from within

ALEX ELLE

SAMPLE ENTRY

I can be	and still
strong	be soft
independent	need support
grieving	find joy
direct	be kind
a leader	need guidance
understanding	have boundaries
creative	need inspiration
a listener	have a voice

Today I affirm:

_____ / _____ / _____

I am	because

Today I affirm:

_____ / /

This	equals this

Today I affirm: ____ / / ____

Love is	Love is not

Today I affirm:

_____ / / _____

In order to	I must

Today I affirm:

_____ / / _____

I can be	and still

today I affirm:

_____ / / _____

I can	without

Today I affirm:

_____ / / _____

I am	even when

Today I affirm:

_____ / _____ / _____

I deserve	despite

Today I affirm: ___/___/___

I am unpacking | and keeping

today I affirm:

_ _ / _ /_

I am worthy | and will not

Today I affirm:

_____ / / _____

I was	now I am

Today I affirm:

_____ / _____ / _____

I choose	I am letting go

Today I affirm:

_____ / / _____

My power is | my weaknesses don't

Today I affirm:

_____ / _____

my flaws are	my shame isn't

Today I affirm:

_ _ / _ / _

I am filled with	I am not lacking

Today I affirm:

I can	with

Today I affirm:

_____ / / _____

I must	in order to

today I affirm:

_____ / / _____

my joy | outweighs

Today I affirm:

_____ / / _____

I need	before

Today I affirm:

_____ / _____ / _____

I require	so that

Today I affirm: _____ / / _____

I am	because

today I affirm:

_____

This	equals this

Today I affirm:

_____ / / _____

Love is	Love is not

Today I affirm:

_____ / / _____

In order to	I must

Today I affirm: _____ / / _____

I can be	and still

Today I affirm:

_____ / /

I can	without

Today I affirm:

_____ / / _____

I am	even when

today I affirm:

_____ / /_____

I deserve | despite

Today I affirm:

_____ / / _____

I am unpacking | and keeping

today I affirm:

_____ / / _____

I am worthy, | and will not

Today I affirm:

_____ / / _____

I was	now I am

today I affirm:

_____ / / _____

I choose	I am letting go

Today I affirm: _/_ _/_ _____

My power is | my weaknesses don't

today I affirm:

_____ / / _____

my flaws are	my shame isn't

Today I affirm:

_____ / / _____

I am filled with	I am not lacking

Today I affirm:

_____ / /

I can   with

Today I affirm:

_____ / _____ /

I must	in order to

today I affirm:

_____ / /

my joy | outweighs

Today I affirm:

_____ / _____ / _____

I need	before

today I affirm:

_____ / / _____

I require	so that

today I affirm:

_____ / / _____

I am	because

Today I affirm:

_____ / / _____

This	equals this

Today I affirm:

_____ / / _____

Love is	Love is not

today I affirm: ___/___/___

In order to	I must

Today I affirm: _____

I can be	and still

today I affirm:

_____ / / _____

I can	without

Today I affirm: __/__/__

I am	even when

today I affirm:

I deserve	despite

Today I affirm:

I am unpacking | and keeping

Today I affirm:

_____ / _____ / _____

I am worthy | and will not

Today I affirm:

_____ / _____ / _____

I was	now I am

Today I affirm:

_____ / _____ /

I choose	I am letting go

Today I affirm:

My power is	my weaknesses don't

113

Today I affirm: ___/___/___

my flaws are	my shame isn't

Today I affirm:

_____ / / _____

I am filled with	I am not lacking

today I affirm: ___/___/___

I can	with

Today I affirm:

_ _ _ / / _

I must	in order to

Today I affirm:

_____ / / _____

my joy | outweighs

Today I affirm:

_____ / / _____

I need	before

today I affirm:

_/ /_

I require	so that

Leaning into my truth validates my journey and makes me whole.

ALEX ELLE

today I affirm

SELF-LOVE LETTERS

My personal self-love journey started with me finding and making time to be kind to myself. Because I'm a writer, I began with a pen and some paper. Some of you may know this as my "Note to Self" exercise. Initially, this task was extremely uncomfortable—but the more I started to pour kindness, compassion, and joy into myself, the more my love notes became a daily practice of gratitude, manifestation, and enjoyment. To get started, refer to the example I have left you. I promise it's not as daunting as it looks. Your love letters can be as long or short as you'd like. Remember, there is not a right or wrong way to complete any of these pages. Move at your own pace! Find your rhythm and create a ritual that best suits you and your evolution through self-care.

Self-worth teaches
me that I
do not have to
lack in order
to provide.

ALEX ELLE

SAMPLE ENTRY

DEAR SELF,

You are _not your mistakes._
you are allowed to misstep, get lost,
and still manage to find your way home.
Failing creates spaces for lessons,
and only you have the power and
wisdom to learn from your shortcomings.

LOVE,
SELF

DEAR SELF,

You are _____

_____

_____

_____

_____

_____

_____

_____

LOVE,
SELF

Today I affirm _____

DEAR SELF,

You can _____

_____

_____

_____

_____

_____

_____

LOVE,
SELF

today I affirm _____

DEAR SELF,

You will _____

_____

_____

_____

_____

_____

_____

LOVE,
SELF

Today I affirm _____

DEAR SELF,

You know _____

_____

_____

_____

_____

_____

LOVE,
SELF

today I affirm _____

DEAR SELF,

You make _____

_____

_____

_____

_____

_____

_____

LOVE,
SELF

Today I affirm _____

DEAR SELF,

You are _____

_____

_____

_____

_____

_____

_____

LOVE,
SELF

today I affirm _____

DEAR SELF,

You can _____

_____

_____

_____

_____

_____

_____

LOVE,
SELF

today I affirm _____

DEAR SELF,

You will _____

_____

_____

_____

_____

_____

LOVE,
SELF

today I affirm _____

DEAR SELF,

You know _____

_____

_____

_____

_____

_____

_____

LOVE,
SELF

Today I affirm _____

DEAR SELF,

You make _____

_____

_____

_____

_____

_____

LOVE,
SELF

today I affirm _____

DEAR SELF,

You are _____

_____

_____

_____

_____

_____

_____

LOVE,
SELF

Today I affirm _____

DEAR SELF,

You can _____

_____

_____

_____

_____

_____

LOVE,
SELF

today I affirm _____

DEAR SELF,

You will _____

_____

_____

_____

_____

_____

_____

LOVE,
SELF

Today I affirm _____

DEAR SELF,

You know _____

_____

_____

_____

_____

_____

_____

LOVE,
SELF

today I affirm _____

DEAR SELF,

YOU make _____

_____

_____

_____

_____

_____

_____

LOVE,
SELF

Today I affirm _____

DEAR SELF,

You are _____

_____

_____

_____

_____

_____

_____

LOVE,
SELF

today I affirm _____

DEAR SELF,

You can _____

_____

_____

_____

_____

_____

_____

LOVE,
SELF

today I affirm _____

DEAR SELF,

You will _____

_____

_____

_____

_____

_____

LOVE,
SELF

today I affirm _____

DEAR SELF,

You know _____

_____

_____

_____

_____

_____

_____

LOVE,
SELF

Today I affirm _____

DEAR SELF,

YOU make _____

_____

_____

_____

_____

_____

_____

LOVE,
SELF

today I affirm _____

DEAR SELF,

You are _____

_____

_____

_____

_____

_____

_____

_____

LOVE,
SELF

Today I affirm _____

DEAR SELF,

You can _____

_____

_____

_____

_____

_____

LOVE,
SELF

today I affirm _____

DEAR SELF,

You will _____

_____

_____

_____

_____

_____

_____

LOVE,
SELF

Today I affirm _____

DEAR SELF,

YOU KNOW _____

_____

_____

_____

_____

_____

_____

LOVE,
SELF

today I affirm _____

DEAR SELF,

YOU make _____

_____

_____

_____

_____

_____

_____

LOVE,
SELF

Today I affirm _____

DEAR SELF,

You are _____

_____

_____

_____

_____

_____

_____

LOVE,
SELF

today I affirm _____

DEAR SELF,

You can _____

_____

_____

_____

_____

_____

_____

**LOVE,
SELF**

Today I affirm _____

DEAR SELF,

You will _____

_____

_____

_____

_____

_____

_____

LOVE,
SELF

today I affirm _____

DEAR SELF,

You know _____

_____

_____

_____

_____

_____

LOVE,
SELF

Today I affirm _____

DEAR SELF,

YOU make _____

_____

_____

_____

_____

_____

LOVE,
SELF

today I affirm _____

___ / ___ / ___

DEAR SELF,

You are _____

_____

_____

_____

_____

_____

_____

_____

LOVE,
SELF

Today I affirm _____

DEAR SELF,

You can _____

_____

_____

_____

_____

_____

_____

LOVE,
SELF

Today I affirm _____

DEAR SELF,

You will _____

_____

_____

_____

_____

_____

_____

LOVE,
SELF

Today I affirm _____

DEAR SELF,

You know _____

_____

_____

_____

_____

_____

_____

LOVE,
SELF

today I affirm _____

DEAR SELF,

You make _____

_____

_____

_____

_____

_____

_____

LOVE,
SELF

Today I affirm _____

DEAR SELF,

You are _____

_____

_____

_____

_____

_____

_____

LOVE,
SELF

today I affirm _____

DEAR SELF,

You can _____

_____

_____

_____

_____

_____

_____

_____

LOVE,
SELF

day I affirm _____

DEAR SELF,

You will _____

_____

_____

_____

_____

_____

_____

LOVE,
SELF

today I affirm _____

DEAR SELF,

YOU KNOW _____

_____

_____

_____

_____

_____

_____

LOVE,
SELF

Today I affirm _____

DEAR SELF,

YOU make _____

_____

_____

_____

_____

_____

_____

LOVE,
SELF

today I affirm _____

DEAR SELF,

You are _____

_____

_____

_____

_____

_____

_____

LOVE,
SELF

Today I affirm _____

DEAR SELF,

You can _____

_____

_____

_____

_____

_____

_____

LOVE,
SELF

today I affirm _____

DEAR SELF,

You will _____

_____

_____

_____

_____

_____

LOVE,
SELF

Today I affirm _____

DEAR SELF,

You know _____

_____

_____

_____

_____

_____

_____

LOVE,
SELF

today I affirm _____

DEAR SELF,

YOU make _____

_____

_____

_____

_____

_____

_____

LOVE,
SELF

today I affirm _____

DEAR SELF,

You are _____

_____

_____

_____

_____

_____

_____

LOVE,
SELF

today I affirm _____

DEAR SELF,

You can _____

_____

_____

_____

_____

_____

_____

LOVE,
SELF

Today I affirm _____

DEAR SELF,

You will _____

_____

_____

_____

_____

_____

_____

LOVE,
SELF

today I affirm _____

DEAR SELF,

You know _____

_____

_____

_____

_____

_____

_____

LOVE,
SELF

Today I affirm _____

DEAR SELF,

You make _____

_____

_____

_____

_____

_____

**LOVE,
SELF**

today I affirm _____

Everything I think
I am lacking
is deep inside
my being;
I just have to
dig for it.

ALEX ELLE

Andrews McMeel Publishing
a division of Andrews McMeel Universal
1130 Walnut Street, Kansas City, Missouri 64106

www.andrewsmcmeel.com

19 20 21 22 23 SDB 10 9 8 7 6 5 4 3 2 1

ISBN: 978-1-4494-9521-3

Library of Congress Control Number: 2018944515

Calligraphy by Josefina Herrera-Sanders

ATTENTION: SCHOOLS AND BUSINESSES
Andrews McMeel books are available at quantity discounts with
bulk purchase for educational, business, or sales promotional use. For information,
please e-mail the Andrews McMeel Publishing Special Sales Department:
specialsales@amuniversal.com.